EVERYDAY
LIFE IN THE
ANCIENT
WORLD

KINGFISHER
Kingfisher Publications Plc
New Penderel House,
283–288 High Holborn,
London WC1V 7HZ
www.kingfisherpub.com

Written by	Julie Ferris, Sue Nicholson, Jonathan Stroud and Sally Tagholm
Consultant	David Nightingale
Editors	Julie Ferris, Camilla Reid and Jonathan Stroud
Designers	Veneta Altham, Mike Buckley, Cormac Jordan, Malcolm Parchment, Jill Plank and Jane Tassie
Illustrations	Inklink Firenze and Kevin Maddison
Editorial Assistance	Prue Grice, Christian Lewis and Katie Puckett
DTP Manager	Nicky Studdart
Production Controllers	Jacquie Horner, Caroline Jackson, Kelly Johnson and Debbie Otter
Picture Research Manager	Jane Lambert
Proofreaders	Sheila Clewley and Emma Wild
Indexer	Kathryn Haig

First published by Kingfisher Publications Plc 2002
1 3 5 7 9 10 8 6 4 2
1TR/1201/TWP/UNI(UNI)/150SMA
Copyright © Kingfisher Publications Plc 2002

A CIP catalogue record for this book is available from
the British Library.

ISBN 0 7534 0682 9

Printed in Singapore

Contents

Contents

Contents

ANCIENT EGYPT

A GUIDE TO EGYPT IN THE TIME OF
RAMESES II, PHARAOH FROM 1289–1224 BC

Introducing Egypt

Visitors to Ancient Egypt will discover a country with a long and fascinating civilization that dates back thousands of years. Its history is divided into different periods – Old Kingdom, Middle Kingdom and New Kingdom. During the New Kingdom, and under the rule of Pharaoh Rameses II, it has become the greatest power in the Middle East.

Sightseers' tip Rameses II's massive construction programme is well under way and looks set to rival the golden age of pyramid building! Make sure you visit the magnificent temples at Karnak and Abu Simbel.

Rameses II came to the throne more than sixty years ago. A renowned soldier, he is famous not only for his many military campaigns, but also for having fathered over 100 children!

Writing was invented nearly 2,000 years before the reign of Rameses II. Hieroglyphs are a combination of ideograms (signs standing for ideas) and phonograms (signs standing for sound).

It was also 2,000 years ago that the tribes of Upper and Lower Egypt were united by the first pharaoh, Menes. His capital was at Memphis.

The first pyramid, the Step Pyramid, was built 1,500 years ago at Saqqara by architect Imhotep as a burial place for Pharaoh Djoser.

The great age of pyramid building lasted for about 400 years. The largest pyramid was built for Pharaoh Khufu at the pyramid complex in Giza.

The most important government official is the vizier, who acts for the pharaoh.

The pharaoh of Egypt is believed to be the god Horus in human form.

The walls of most monuments and temples are covered in hieroglyphs.

Most major attractions are situated in the Nile Valley, a fertile area known as "Black Land". The desert, which lies to the east and west, is called "Red Land" and is largely uninhabited.

The beautiful city of Thebes, capital of Egypt since the reign of Mentuhotep II, is within easy reach of many of the most popular tourist attractions. It is a busy and bustling city with lots to see, including magnificent temples, palaces and obelisks.

Five hundred years ago, Egyptian pharaohs conquered Nubia, pushing Egypt's empire 320 km south. Egyptian rule was imposed and forts, temples and towns were built. Huge quantities of gold are extracted from Nubian mines.

Tutankhamun, the "boy king", came to the throne 70 years ago, aged ten. He died nine years later and his body is believed to be buried in the Valley of the Kings, in a tomb full of spectacular treasures.

The Egyptian empire is currently at its height. Pharaoh Rameses II has fought many brave battles and ordered the construction of many monuments across Egypt.

Travelling around

Boat trips on Egypt's main artery, the River Nile, are an ideal way to see the sights, as well as the beautiful and varied wildlife. Watch out for small cargo boats bulging with grain, broad cattle vessels packed with livestock and huge ships transporting gigantic granite columns and obelisks. You may even see one of the famous funeral barges that ferry the mummies of wealthy citizens to holy burial grounds.

Most people get around on foot in town, but if you are feeling lazy, treat yourself to a ride on a palanquin, or carrying chair, just like the pharaoh.

Be prepared to haggle for your boat trip – prices vary according to the time of year.

The Nile is full of crocodiles, so check that your boat is watertight!

The heat is intense so always take plenty of water with you when you travel.

Sightseers' tip

If you are planning a long expedition into the desert, it is advisable to hire a donkey. Available in most towns, they are cheap but extremely reliable.

Intrepid travellers will enjoy a day trip to the desert that lies to the east and the west of the Nile valley. The "Red Land", has a harsh and mysterious landscape that covers more than 90 percent of the entire country. Make sure that you are accompanied by an experienced guide, or join one of the many merchants' caravans travelling the trade routes to the coast.

It can get very hot in the Egyptian sun. Make sure you travel on a boat with some kind of canopy or awning to provide shade in the intense heat.

Boats are the main form of transport in Egypt and most people live close to the river. Usually made from papyrus or wood, many boats have a central sail.

What to wear

Pack the bare minimum – with daytime temperatures well over 30°C, you won't need many clothes. What you do take should be light and comfortable. A simple, white linen shift is ideal for everyday wear in town. In the country, people usually wear just a loincloth.

You will find exquisite golden jewellery made by highly skilled craftsmen. It is often inlaid with semi-precious stones from the desert, or imported stones such as turquoise.

Most people go barefoot but it is a good idea to buy a pair of plaited papyrus sandals to protect your feet from scorpions and snakes.

Sightseers' tip

Both men and women wear a thick black eye paint known as kohl. It is made from ground minerals and kept in elaborate cosmetic jars.

Pleats and fringes are the latest New Kingdom fashion with men wearing long, pleated skirts over a short underkilt, and women wearing pleated robes of the finest white linen gauze.

You will need valuable objects if you wish to barter for Egyptian jewellery.

Egyptians rub their skin with cat, crocodile and hippopotamus fat.

Magical charms are worn on necklaces to prevent sickness.

For evening wear it is important to dress in more elaborate outfits, especially if you are invited to a banquet or feast. On formal occasions both men and women wear dazzling jewellery, and braided black wigs made of human hair and held in place with beeswax. Perfumes made from oils scented with myrrh and cinammon are popular.

Flax plants provide the linen for all Egyptian clothes – from the coarsest material to the finest gauze.

Food and drink

The wide selection of food stalls in most towns means that it is easy to get a takeaway. Bread, fruit, vegetables and beans are available to visitors on a tight budget, and delicious dried fish and wild birds are on offer to the more adventurous. Meat is very expensive and is only eaten on special occasions.

The thick, lumpy beer is made from mashed barley bread, so use a syphon!

Bread comes in all shapes and sizes. The flour is made by grinding grain between two stones.

If you are lucky enough to be invited to a banquet, you will see that wealthy Egyptians eat very well indeed. There are dozens of courses, and the menu might include duck, goose and ox, as well as delicacies such as gazelle, antelope and ostrich.

The host and important guests usually sit on low chairs or stools. Other people use mats or cushions on the floor.

Spices and herbs, like cumin, mustard and thyme are often used to flavour meals.

Watch out! Grit in the flour used to make bread might break a tooth!

Always check before eating fish – it is considered sacred in some areas!

Don't worry about knives and forks – everyone in Egypt eats with their fingers, rinsing their hands between courses. You may notice that banquet guests often wear cones of perfumed fat on their heads. These melt during the evening, keeping them cool.

Sightseers' tip

Although beer is the national drink, why not try one of the many fine Egyptian wines? Local date or palm wines are excellent value.

Accommodation

A wide variety of accommodation to suit most budgets is available in all major cities. You can choose between a luxury suite in a nobleman's house, a room in an attractive town house or a cheap and cheerful stay in a poorer quarter.

Sightseers' tip Windows should be small and high to keep out the heat and dust. Houses are often built on raised platforms as many areas are badly affected by the Nile floods.

Cheap accommodation can be somewhat cramped, with several families living together. Be prepared to share a room and to sleep on the floor or on the roof.

Beds, chairs, tables and chests are usually carved out of a local wood like sycamore fig. However, cheap accommodation has little furniture.

If you are on a tight budget, why not stay out of town? Tomb-workers' village houses are simple, but excellent value. Animals are often stabled in the front room, but you can sleep on the roof.

Don't expect to sleep well. Egyptians use wooden headrests as pillows!

Grand houses have tiled floors and coloured ceilings and walls.

Cooking is done outside to reduce fire risk in cheap accommodation.

Top of the range rooms are available all year round in country villas owned by noble families. Cool and comfortable, they offer every amenity, including bathrooms! You will enjoy Egyptian hospitality at its best, including lavish home-made food. You can also relax in tranquil gardens by a pool brimming with fish and lotus flowers.

All Egyptian houses, from the pharaoh's spectacular palace to the humblest village home, are made of mud bricks. The mud is mixed with chopped straw, shaped into moulds and baked in the sun.

Shopping

A visit to one of Egypt's bustling markets can provide a welcome break from sightseeing. It is essential to make a day of it if you pick one of the major centres like Memphis or Thebes, and you are guaranteed to find an amazing variety of produce and goods. Mouth-watering pomegranates, melons and figs, sticky sweetmeats, olives, dates and over 30 different kinds of bread are all readily available.

Large town markets can be very hot and noisy, with traders bringing in their wares from far and wide. Shopping can take a long time – stall-holders are well trained in the art of bartering!

Egyptian craftsmen produce beautiful vases, statues and carvings in stone, wood, metal and ivory.

If you are thirsty there are always plenty of beer stalls to choose from.

You will find beautiful crafts for sale in palace and temple workshops.

Leave your money at home – Egyptians use a bartering system instead!

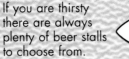 **Sightseers' tip** "Sniffer" baboons are a common sight in many markets. They play a vital role in the fight against crime, helping officials track down thieves.

The markets are also a very good place to shop for crafts and clothes – the kingdom has a reputation for producing the finest linen in the world! With its long history of trading with other nations, Egypt also buys a huge range of exotic goods, such as precious stones and olive oil, from neighbouring countries. If you visit one of the smaller country markets, remember that you will find only home-grown produce and locally made artefacts.

You will soon get used to the bartering system and will quickly be able to work out exactly how many fig cakes equal a gold necklace. Market officials are always on hand to sort out any disputes between traders.

Leisure time

Whether you are young or old, there is a wide range of leisure activities on offer. If possible, try to time your visit to coincide with one of the major religious festivals, which often last for several days. You can be sure of a spectacular show with acrobats, jugglers, dancers and vibrant music.

Egyptian children play with all sorts of different toys including dolls, model animals and spinning tops. They also enjoy playing catch with balls made of clay.

Egyptians love children – you will see them playing everywhere. Don't be surprised by the latest hairstyle. All boys up to 12 years of age have "side-locks".

Egypt's rich cultural heritage is reflected in the ancient art of story telling, which is handed down from generation to generation. Sit down quietly in the shade and listen to a story about the exploits of the gods, or the adventures of a crocodile in the Nile!

It is said that Pharaoh Tutankhamun's tomb has four senet boards in it.

Hathor is goddess of happiness, dance and music, as well as love.

Some stories may be familiar – Cinderella is an Egyptian tale!

Sightseers' tip The biggest festival takes place at New Year (usually around 19th July). It marks the first glimpse of Sirius, the "Dog Star", and there is a five-day national holiday.

You can always try your hand at one of the many Egyptian board-games such as snake, which is played on a circular stone board, or senet. Leapfrog and tug-of-war are also popular games.

Music is everywhere! Musicians perform on string, wind and percussion instruments at festivals and banquets. Farmers even sing to their oxen as they thresh the corn!

Senet, one of the most popular board-games, is played with counters and small sticks. There are 30 squares which you have to cross, overcoming evils and obstacles, to reach the kingdom of Osiris.

21

Hunting

Unchanged since the earliest days of Egyptian civilization, the traditional hippo hunt on the River Nile makes for a thrilling excursion. Alternatively, hunting trips in the desert, once reserved for kings and courtiers, are now widely available to travellers.

Teams of hunters in papyrus boats chase huge hippos through the water. They use lassoes to catch them and spears to weaken them.

Egyptian nobles often take their wives and children with them when they go hunting.

 Lion hunting is banned during the festival of the cat, when the god Bast is worshipped.

Make sure your arrows are sharp. They should be tipped with ivory, bone, flint or metal.

Sightseers' tip Hunting birds in the reed thickets of the River Nile is a popular activity. Hire of a boat is optional, but a sturdy wooden throwstick is essential.

Cats are considered sacred and often wear a golden ring. Domesticated during the Middle Kingdom, they are now used by hunters to help them catch birds and wildlife. The Egyptian word for cat is "Miw".

If you go hunting for desert hare, wild bull, gazelle, oryx, antelope or lion, make sure you are properly equipped. Bring plenty of javelins, spears and arrows, which you can store in your horse-drawn chariot. Never hunt in the desert without an experienced guide and at least one hunting dog.

23

Mummification

Egyptians believe in life after death and preserve the body by mummification. Head for the west bank of the Nile and visit one of the funerary workshops where bodies are prepared for their tombs and the journey to the next world.

As the layers of linen are wrapped round a mummy, amulets are bound in for good luck. They help to make the journey to the next world as smooth as possible.

The body is covered with natron (a compound of sodium and carbon) and left to dry for at least 40 days before being bandaged in linen.

The lungs, stomach, liver and intestines are removed from the body, dried and wrapped in linen. They are stored separately in canopic jars, which are placed in the tomb. The heart is cleaned and wrapped and returned to the body, but the brain is extracted through the nose and then thrown away!

24

Coffins are richly decorated with gods of the underworld and hieroglyphs of spells.

The heart is left in the body for judgement in the afterlife.

Egyptians take everything they will need in the afterlife with them to the tomb!

Sightseers' tip Don't forget that the Egyptians have an unshakeable belief in magic. Any part of your body can be used in a spell against you!

A huge industry has sprung up with a sliding scale of charges depending on requirements. The treatments range from the basic (injecting the body with cedar oil so that the insides drain out) to top-of-the-range mummification, which includes the finest linen gauze bandages, bags of exotic spices and the inclusion of semi-precious jewels.

Mummification is not reserved exclusively for humans. Cats, dogs and even crocodiles often get the same treatment – complete with animal-shaped coffins and painted faces.

25

The pyramids

The three great pyramids at Giza are not only Egypt's top tourist attraction, they are also regarded as some of the greatest feats of engineering the world has ever known. They were built more than 1,200 years before the reign of Rameses II as burial tombs for pharaohs Khufu, Khafre and Menkure.

Sightseers' tip

"Tomb robber tours" are the only way to see inside the pyramids. You will be taken through huge granite doors and along a network of secret corridors and false passages.

Don't miss the famous Step Pyramid at Saqqara – the first pyramid ever built in Egypt. Designed by the great architect, Imhotep, it is the burial place of Pharaoh Djoser.

The angles of the walls of the Bent Pyramid of Pharaoh Sneferu at Dahshur change towards the top, giving the pyramid its distinctive shape.

Granite was brought by river from Aswan, and white limestone was ferried across the Nile.

 Many pyramids have inscriptions of magic spells to aid the journey to the afterlife.

The huge pyramid of Pharaoh Khufu took more than twenty years to build!

At 138 metres high, Khufu's pyramid is the largest stone building on Earth, and is one of the Seven Wonders of the World. It is made up of more than 2.3 million limestone blocks, each weighing at least 2.5 tonnes!

The casing of polished limestone, which gives the pyramids their smooth sides, has begun to erode.

The Great Sphinx, which guards the pyramids at Giza, has a lion's body and the face of Pharaoh Khafre. Made of stone, it is 73 metres long and 20 metres high.

Farmers helped to build the pyramids during the annual floods. They used simple copper and stone tools to cut the massive blocks of stone. These were hauled up mud and brick ramps on wooden sledges.

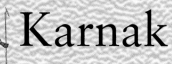

Karnak

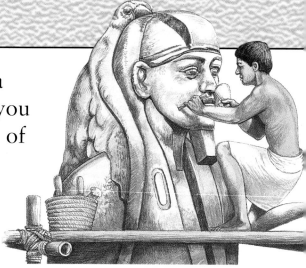

Make an early start and take a sturdy pair of sandals with you when you visit the famous Temple of Amun at Karnak, just north of Thebes. Karnak has grown over the centuries from a modest shrine to a vast temple complex. The most recent addition has only just been completed – the spectacular Hypostyle Hall has 134 gigantic pillars, each one carved and brightly decorated to look like a huge papyrus plant.

You will probably notice that the colossal statues of Rameses II currently being erected are of a scale and splendour unrivalled in previous dynasties. Finishing touches are chiselled by skilled masons.

Overlooking the Nile at Abu Simbel, an enormous temple for Rameses has been cut deep into the sandstone cliffs. It has been designed so that twice a year the rays of the Sun illuminate a statue of Rameses inside.

If you visit Karnak during the annual religious festival, you might catch a glimpse of the statue of Amun, king of all the gods. This is the one time it leaves its home deep inside the sanctuary to visit another temple.

Stroll up an avenue of ram-headed sphinxes to reach the temple's great sloping walls, covered with stunning pictures of the gods.

Amun is shown as a ram, a goose or a serpent, but most often as a crowned king.

The obelisks are capped with gold and covered with prayers to the gods.

 You may not be allowed in the temple itself – it is usually reserved for priests.

Karnak is the most important religious centre in the whole of Egypt. It is known as Ipet-isut – "the most perfect of places". The vast complex includes workshops, living-quarters, a school, a library, a sacred pool and storehouses.

Sightseers' tip Egyptians often pray to statues of the pharaoh. This is because they believe he is descended from the gods.

An Egyptian farm

Farming is the basis of Egypt's thriving economy, with a wide variety of fruit and vegetables being cultivated on the fertile banks of the Nile. If you plan to visit a farm, make sure you avoid the inundation season (July to November), when the river floods and most of the fields are under water.

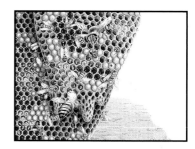

Honey is widely used as a sweetener in Egypt, and many farms have beehives.

Don't miss Egypt's famous wine-growing area in the north of the kingdom.

Travelling around is tiring. You may prefer to stay at a farm overnight!

Thanksgiving ceremonies are held at the height of the floods.

Farming methods are simple but extremely efficient. Crops include wheat and barley (to make bread and beer) and flax (to make linen).

Sightseers' tip If you visit a farm during the ploughing or harvest seasons, you might get roped in to lend a hand!

A "shaduf" is used to raise water from the Nile to fill irrigation canals. It has a bucket on one end and a weight on the other to aid lifting.

Along with mouth-watering fruits and vegetables such as melons, pomegranates, figs, onions, garlic and beans, farmers often keep cattle, sheep and pigs. Birds, including ducks and geese, are also reared for eggs and meat.

Be prepared for hard work if you go on a fishing trip on the Nile. Fishermen use small boats made of bundles of papyrus reed tied together with twine. Their fishing nets, also made of papyrus, are weighted down with stones or lead.

Survival guide

Plan your holiday carefully before you travel and make sure you have all essential documents. You may be refused entry to this highly bureaucratic country if your paperwork is not in order! If there is a problem, ask to see the local scribe. He will be able to draw up any document you need for a small fee.

Administration

The pharaoh is not only the king of Egypt, but also thought to be Horus, son of the sun god Re. He holds absolute civil, religious and military power. However, since the New Kingdom years have brought great military expansion, he has delegated a lot of day-to-day administration to various government departments.

You'll only see scribes writing hieroglyphs on tomb and temple walls or in important matters of state. Everyday Egyptian – a simple, joined-up version – is much easier to learn!

Law and order

Many documents carry seals made by rings carved with sacred symbols. Official documents always carry the seal of Rameses II to prove that they are authentic.

Local police keep order in most towns. However, if you are planning to venture alone into the countryside or desert, you should be wary of robbers. In Egypt, justice is carefully administered – by the vizier in the great courtrooms of the capital, and by local people in the village courts. The most common form of punishment is beating.

The pharaoh travels all over Egypt to inspect local projects and take part in ceremonies.

Remember – hieroglyphs can be written from left to right, right to left, or top to bottom.

If you don't win in court, you can always appeal to the local god!

Health

Egyptian doctors are highly skilled and have a detailed knowledge of anatomy. They work closely with magicians when practising medicine. Common injuries like snake bites and scorpion stings are most effectively treated with a combination of spells and medicines. Garlic is a very valuble plant, as it has both medical and magical powers.

If you want extra protection from the evil spirits that cause disease, you could invest in a magical charm, or amulet. The eye of Horus is believed to be particularly powerful.

❓ Souvenir quiz

At the end of your stay in Egypt, your suitcase is probably full of exotic souvenirs! Have a go at this quiz to test your knowledge of Ancient Egypt. You will find the answers on page 128.

1. There are many different ways to get around in Ancient Egypt. What is the pharaoh's favourite form of transport?

a) He likes to ride on a small grey donkey.

b) He travels on a large cattle vessel on the Nile.

c) He prefers to be carried about in a palanquin, or carrying chair.

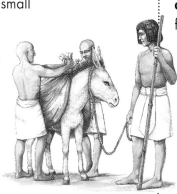

2. Ordinary Egyptian furniture, such as beds and chairs, is usually carved out of which sort of wood?

a) Ebony inlaid with gold and semi-precious stones.

b) Locally grown sycamore fig.

c) Cedar wood which is imported from Lebanon or Syria.

3. Although many Egyptians go barefoot, cool and comfortable sandals are often worn. What are they made of?

a) They are made using locally grown fringed flax.

b) The sandals are made of plaited papyrus, palm fibre or leather.

c) Egyptians wear braided human hair and beeswax sandals.

4. Mummification is increasingly popular in New Kingdom Egypt – for humans as well as some cats and crocodiles! Where are the bodies prepared?

a) Funerary workshops on the west bank of the Nile.

b) The pyramids at Giza.

c) The oasis city of Crocodilopolis.

5. Some of the pyramids are lined with hieroglyphic inscriptions. What are they?

a) Directions to the pharaoh's burial chamber deep inside the pyramid.

b) Official government warning to tomb robbers to stay away from the pyramid.

c) Magical spells to help the pharaoh's body rise to the skies and arrive safely in the afterlife.

6. You will certainly have visited some of Rameses II's spectacular new buildings, which include an exciting addition to the Temple of Amun at Karnak. What is it?

a) The Temple of Amun at Luxor.

b) Colossal gold-capped obelisks inscribed with hieroglyphs.

c) The Hypostyle Hall with its stunning 134 gigantic, painted columns.

7. Although Rameses II holds absolute civil, religious and military power, he has been forced to delegate some authority. Who is second-in-command?

a) Horus, the son of Re, the sun god in human form.

b) The chief minister, or vizier.

c) A trained magician who has detailed knowledge of spells and the properties of plants.

8. You will probably have tried your hand at one of the many board games enjoyed by Egyptians, young and old. Which of these popular games was buried with Tutankhamun?

a) Senet – using counters and a throwstick, you have to overcome obstacles and evils to reach the kingdom of Osiris.

b) Snake – using small stone balls, you have to reach the centre of a circular board, coiled in the shape of a serpent.

c) Pythons and pyramids – an ancient version of snakes and ladders.

ANCIENT GREECE

A GUIDE TO GREECE IN 432 BC DURING ITS GOLDEN AGE

Introducing Greece

There has never been a better time to visit Ancient Greece. Made up of small, independent city-states around the Mediterranean coast, Greece is currently experiencing a cultural golden age. The relative peace between the often warring cities has allowed the arts, theatre, politics, philosophy and science to flourish.

Athens is a democracy and one if its most influential statesmen is Pericles. He is usually portrayed wearing a helmet and is rumoured to have a slightly misshapen head.

Sightseers' tip   The city-state of Athens would make a good base for your holiday. It has an impressive political system, and the recently built Parthenon temple on the Acropolis is well worth a visit.

Over 800 years before the Golden Age, Mycenaeans lived in Greece. They were famed for their gold treasures.

Greeks began to venture out from their homeland and to establish colonies around the coasts of the Mediterranean.

The first Olympic Games were held 270 years before the Golden Age. Around the same time, writing was developed.

For most of the year Greece is mild, but in summer it is very hot and dusty.

A city-state comprises the city itself and the countryside surrounding it.

Female travellers beware – women are rarely allowed out of the home.

Dominating the Athens skyline is the Acropolis. Once a hilltop fort, it is now a holy place with stunning temples. Athens is the largest and most powerful of the Greek city-states and has a population of about 250,000.

Athens is ruled by democracy, which means that all male citizens can take part in the government of the city. This freedom of speech means that relations between the rich and poor are considerably better than in other city-states. Citizens have a say in the running of the city and therefore do not resent the wealthy landowners. However, some aristocrats complain that they are not given enough respect, and that the poor don't move out of their way in the streets! Other city-states, such as Sparta, are ruled by kings or small groups of aristocrats.

A system of democracy evolved in Athens. All male citizens are given a say in how the state is governed.

For ten years before the Golden Age began, Greece was locked in war with Persia, a middle eastern empire.

Athens' victory in the Persian Wars reinvigorates Greek culture, and the Acropolis is rebuilt.

Travelling around

The Greeks are considered great sailors, and if you attempt to cross the mountainous inland regions you will discover why. To avoid a long, steep trek by donkey, board one of the many ships that arrive and depart from Athens' famous harbour, Piraeus.

If you want to travel inland, hire a donkey to make the journey less tiring. Make sure you wear a wide-brimmed straw hat to protect you from the hot sun.

Big eyes are painted on the sides of the prow of Greek ships to scare away evil spirits and protect the sailors.

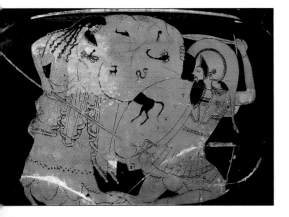

Ancient Greece is made up of many different islands and the only way to travel from one island to another is by boat. Sailing is also a good way to get to coastal towns around the mainland.

Poseidon, the god of the sea, carries a trident – a spear with three prongs. Greeks believe he has the power to prevent shipwrecks and make offerings of wine to him.

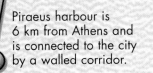
Piraeus harbour is 6 km from Athens and is connected to the city by a walled corridor.

Avoid travelling on merchant ships. They are slow and easily captured by pirates.

Greek sailors like to keep sight of the coast and will not sail in bad weather.

Avoid visiting Greece during the winter months when travel practically comes to a halt. Winters tend to be very wet, making mountain tracks impassable. Sailing also becomes difficult because boat sails get wet and visibility is poor.

Sightseers' tip
Along the rough, stony roads inland are inns and shops for travellers. However, their reputation is not good. Comedy writers often include jokes about cheating innkeepers in their plays!

What to wear

To look the part in Athens you can't go wrong with a simple chiton (pronounced "kye-ton"). Made from linen or wool, the chiton is little more than a tube of material pinned or sewn over the shoulders. Over the chiton Greeks drape a hard-wearing woollen cloak called a himation.

To take a shower, Greeks sit in a large pottery bowl while a slave pours cool water over them.

Sightseers' tip

It is a sign of good breeding and elegance to have your himation arranged correctly. If it is too short, your neighbours will laugh at you, too long and it will drag in the mud. Himations are expensive to make and are a popular target for thieves.

You can buy clothes in the market, but they are expensive!

Look out for girls wearing high-heeled sandals to make them taller.

Greeks don't wear underwear. If you are cold put on another chiton.

Women wear their chitons to the ankle and dye them bright colours such as red, yellow, green and purple.

Greek women are rarely allowed to leave the house. When they do they wear their finest jewellery. Hairpins, rings and earrings can be purchased from travelling pedlars.

Make sure you visit a barber shop while in Athens. It is a popular place to meet and exchange news and gossip. Greek men tend to keep their hair short and most have beards. Women tie their long hair up in carefully arranged styles. Blonde hair is greatly admired and many women have tried using bleach.

Although Greeks go barefoot in the home, comfy leather sandals are worn in the street. You can have them custom made by a cobbler. He will ask you to stand on the leather while he draws around your foot.

It is very fashionable for women to have pale skin. Poor women have suntans from working outside and often paint their faces with white lead to look paler. Be warned! The lead can bring you out in a rash, or even kill you if you use too much.

Food and drink

Unless you are dining with aristocrats, food in Ancient Greece tends to be quite basic and the meals informal. Meat is very expensive and the poor only eat it at religious festivals.

Sightseers' tip

Professional cooks are hired for symposions. Slaves are sent out with invitations – small statues showing people eating or walking to a feast.

Dinner parties, called symposions, are very popular in aristocratic circles. The guests lie on couches and enjoy a lavish three-course meal. Dishes can include piglet stuffed with thrushes, egg yolks with oysters, and quinces cooked in honey and baked in a tart.

 Greeks eat meals outdoors during the day. Evening meals are eaten at sunset.

 Animals are sacrificed at religious festivals and offerings of food and wine are made.

 Peasants drink goat's milk or water. Wine is often diluted.

Wine is drunk from a broad, shallow cup called a kylix. Drinking games are popular at symposions.

 Women prepare all the food. Cooking is done over a charcoal fire and bronze or clay utensils are used.

Slaves at the symposion dinner will cut up your food for you, and sometimes even feed you. After the meal, acrobats, dancing girls and musicians perform for the guests and vast quantities of wine are drunk. Stories and jokes are told, and very often politics is discussed. Female visitors, however, are unlikely to be invited to a symposion. The only women allowed to attend are slaves and entertainers.

Bread, gruel, olives, figs and cheese made from goat's milk are the most common foods. Cheap, fresh fish is available in coastal towns.

Accommodation

To fully experience Ancient Greece, stay as a guest in a typical Greek house. They are made of mud bricks and have tiled roofs. The rooms are all on one floor and are built around an open-air courtyard where women relax and chat to one another, the family eats its meals, and children play.

Sightseers' tip

Keep your valuables safe! The mud bricks are quite soft and it is easy for burglars to cut through the walls!

Most Greek households have slaves. Male slaves guard the house and do the shopping. Female slaves do the cooking and cleaning.

Three-legged furniture is very common. It can stand on any surface, even bumpy earth floors.

As wood is scarce in mountainous Greece, most houses are poorly furnished.

 Many houses contain a small shrine in the courtyard where you can worship the gods.

Greeks use large pots as toilets, which slaves have to empty every day.

Clay oil lamps are lit at night. Oil is poured in the middle and a wick is placed in the spout.

Greek women are only allowed to leave their homes for short periods of time. They are not even supposed to open the outer door of the house in case they come face to face with a man. While boys are at school, girls learn to run the house by helping their mothers.

47

Shopping

The best place for shopping in Athens, as in any Greek city-state, is the agora, or market-place. Everything from meat, fish, vegetables and fruit, to pottery, bronze ware and textiles is available from the market stalls and shops. You will even be able to buy slaves! The agora is the centre of Athenian life and men spend most of their day there.

Why not commission a sculptor to make you a statue of a god to bring you luck?

There are no pockets in Greek clothing – it is customary to carry coins in your mouth.

Religious and political speakers can often be found at the agora.

Sightseers' tip

At the agora you will find finely carved marble figures and bronze statues. Pottery bowls, vases and cups decorated with scenes of Greek life and paintings of gods and heroes are also available.

The most common Athenian coin has a picture of Athena, goddess of the city, on one side. On the other side is her emblem, an owl.

If it gets too hot in the middle of the day, why not take a stroll round the stoa, the sheltered colonnade on the edges of the agora? Shoemakers, ironmongers, carpenters, money-lenders and doctors are all to be found in the stoa, as well as the offices of lawyers and magistrates.

In the stoa you may well see a philosopher explaining his ideas, or a storyteller recounting tales of the gods and heroes. The most famous stories, the *Iliad* and the *Odyssey*, describe the war between Greece and Troy.

49

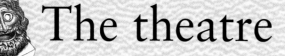

The theatre

No trip to Ancient Greece would be complete without a visit to the theatre. The semicircular theatre in Athens can hold over 10,000 people and entry costs two obols. Performances are held once a month, and last all day. However, make sure you get there early – the theatre is usually full by dawn! If you enjoy serious drama, you could watch a Greek tragedy. If you prefer boisterous, and often vulgar, entertainment, go and see a comedy.

If you get bored between plays, make use of one of the game boards scratched on some of the seats.

Sightseers' tip

Show your appreciation by whistling and stamping your feet. Don't get too rowdy – theatre staff may beat you with a stick!

 Bring plenty to eat and drink as the performances last all day.

 Drama was invented in Athens as part of the spring festival for the god Dionysus.

 Look out for the important officials who sit in ceremonial seats at the front.

No more than three actors in each play take the various speaking roles, changing masks to show which character they are playing. A chorus of around 15 actors sings or chants parts of the story. Although women are allowed to go to the theatre, all roles in the plays, including female ones, are played by men.

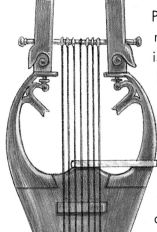

Plays often include music. The lyre, which is similar to a harp, is the most popular instrument. You will also see musicians playing the double flute. It is difficult to play as it requires twice as much breath as a single flute.

The assembly

Athens is a democracy, and every Athenian citizen has a say in the running of the city. Important matters are debated and decided at the assembly. This is held, on average, every nine days on the slopes of the Pynx Hill. There have to be at least 6,000 citizens at each assembly.

To prevent anyone speaking for too long during a debate, speeches are timed with a water clock.

Sightseers' tip

Make sure you arrive in good time. Those who are slow to enter the assembly are forced to hurry. A rope dipped in red paint herds people in. If you dawdle you will get paint on your clothes and have to pay a fine.

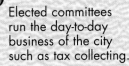

Women and slaves are not allowed to speak or vote at an assembly.

Elected committees run the day-to-day business of the city such as tax collecting.

Speeches can be very entertaining and speakers often taunt each other.

Although anyone is allowed to stand up and make a speech, it is so daunting that usually only the well-educated dare to do it. Rival speakers jeer at each other and try to persuade the crowd that their ideas are the best. Slave archers keep order in case a discussion becomes rowdy. When a matter has been fully debated, citizens vote by raising their hands.

Juries vote by dropping bronze ballots with hollow (guilty) or solid (innocent) shafts into a box. By holding the ballot between finger and thumb, you can stop people seeing which way you vote.

The atmosphere at trials in Athens is often tense and the trials are usually rowdy as jurors are allowed to shout questions at the defendants or prosecutors. The juries are very large – sometimes thousands in important cases. This makes them difficult to bribe. After all the evidence has been heard, the jurors vote for whoever they feel has presented the most convincing argument.

53

The Acropolis

One of the most picturesque attractions that Athens has to offer is the Acropolis, or "highest city". Built originally as a fortress, the Acropolis has recently been redeveloped. At its centre is a splendid new temple called the Parthenon.

Sightseers' tip

The columns of the Parthenon were designed by the architect, Iktinos, to taper slightly at the top so that they look straight when viewed from a distance. If they had been built straight, optical illusion would have made them seem too thin in the middle.

Built by Athenians to celebrate the end of the long wars against Persia, the Parthenon is dedicated to Athena, patron of the city and goddess of wisdom and war. It is built from dazzling, white marble and filled with statues and fine carvings.

There is a large family of gods, each with different powers. Apollo is god of the arts, Aphrodite is goddess of love and Zeus is king of all the gods.

 If you can't afford to give an animal sacrifice at the temple, offer a pastry sacrifice instead.

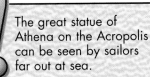 The great statue of Athena on the Acropolis can be seen by sailors far out at sea.

 Athena is believed to have been born fully formed from Zeus's forehead.

Friezes in the Parthenon commemorate the Panathenaia festival, held every July in honour of Athena. There is singing, dancing, athletics and a temple procession.

There are no weekends in Ancient Greece, so people look forward particularly to the 40 religious festivals held each year in Athens. As well as time off work, there is always a lot of free food, drink and entertainment on offer during festivals.

Look out for one of these coin-operated water dispensers when you visit the Parthenon temple.

The Olympic Games

The gods are believed to live in the clouds above Mount Olympus. Although named after the mountain, Olympia is a long way from it.

Try to time your visit to Ancient Greece to coincide with the Olympic Games in Olympia. They are held every four years in honour of Zeus, king of the gods, and are open to athletes from all over Greece. Events include running, chariot racing, long jump, javelin, discus and fighting.

There is a luxury hotel for officials, but most visitors sleep in the open.

 The Games are held every four years in July, and admission is free.

Make sure you see the massive gold and ivory statue of Zeus at Olympia.

The fiercest event at the Games is the pankration, a cross between boxing and wrestling. Only eye-gouging and biting are against the rules.

The Games are taken very seriously. Even in times of war a truce is declared so that the Games can go ahead.

Sightseers' tip Because the athletes compete naked, women are not allowed to watch under any circumstance. However, they hold their own games in honour of the goddess Hera, wife of Zeus.

The stadium has room for about 40,000 spectators. Only the judges have seats, so you will have to stand or sit on the surrounding hillside. Dancers and jugglers entertain the crowds in between events, and there are food stalls for refreshments. Remember, wearing a hat is forbidden in case it blocks someone's view.

Winners are presented with a wreath of olive leaves cut from a sacred tree.

Sparta

The city-state of Sparta in southern Greece is a fascinating place to visit. In contrast to the rest of Greece, Sparta's entire culture is based on maintaining its full-time army. Citizens are forbidden to work and there are no holidays. Life in Sparta is an endless cycle of military drills and exercises.

Bravery is very important to the Spartans. You will have no problem identifying a coward. Half his hair and half his beard are shaved off and he is jeered at in the street.

Spartan citizens have to do 23 years' compulsory military training. Land slaves called helots work the fields and feed the Spartans. The helots are treated very cruelly.

You may not want to stay long – by Athenian standards, life in Sparta is very tough and dull.

Weak and sickly babies are taken to the mountains and left to die.

Spartans eat a black broth made of pork, stock, vinegar and salt.

One of the first things you'll see when you arrive in Sparta is a group of men or boys training for war. Spartans have little family life. They believe that warriors should be loyal to their community and not to their relations. Boys are sent to military school at the age of seven, and they live and train in the barracks until their military service ends.

Women in Sparta are expected to exercise and keep fit so that they will produce strong, healthy babies.

Spartans learn to move stealthily in the dark, to steal food and to live with few clothes or possessions. They are not encouraged to read books for fear that they will develop their own ideas.

Sightseers' tip

Spartan soldiers are very organized and disciplined. You may see Spartan men marching in a formation called a phalanx – side by side in tight rows.

59

The countryside

Most Athenians own small-holdings in the country. Even though there is not much fertile soil, the Greeks make the most of the land and grow fig trees, vines, olive trees, wheat and barley. The land owner and his slaves do all the work by hand.

Fishing is very important in Greece. Trawling nets are used out at sea, and fishing rods are used in rivers and lakes.

Sightseers' tip

Rather than pick olives one by one from a tree, farmers beat the branches with a stick to make the ripe fruit fall to the floor. Then the olives are put in a press and the oil is squeezed from them.

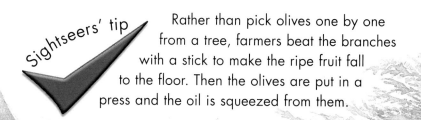

Olive oil is sometimes presented as a prize to athletes at the Olympic Games.

A lot of food is imported into Greece. Eels from Boeotia are a favourite in Athens.

The oracle at Delphi is the richest and most powerful oracle in Greece.

The priestess at Delphi speaks to the gods when she is in a trance. The gods communicate with her in riddles which are translated by the priests.

Make sure you visit the temple at Delphi when you are travelling around the countryside. At the temple, which is dedicated to Apollo, you can, for a sum of money, consult the oracle (a priestess who speaks to the gods on your behalf) and discover what the future holds for you. Greek cities often consult the oracle at Delphi for political advice.

Survival guide

Visitors to Ancient Greece may find it difficult to travel around. Not only is there much rivalry between the different city-states, there is also a general dislike of foreigners as Greeks consider themselves to be culturally superior. Take care – many outsiders end up as slaves!

Health

Health care in Ancient Greece is very sophisticated. If you have cause to visit a doctor you will be asked what your symptoms are, what sort of food you eat and whether you take exercise. Once the doctor has all relevant information written down, he will prescribe a herbal cure. Health is considered the greatest gift of the gods to man.

Greek doctors are generally well-dressed, cheerful and highly knowledgeable. One doctor, Hippocrates of Cos, has written down the methods a doctor must follow.

Administration

Most Greek boys learn how to read and write. Ink is made from soot or taken from cuttlefish, and bark or papyrus are commonly used as paper. Many walls have carved inscriptions.

The main units of money are the obol and the drachma (worth about six obols). Visitors will soon be familiar with half-obol, obol, drachma and two- and four-drachma coins. Citizens in Athens earn about half a drachma a day. Units of length are the finger (19.3 mm) and the foot. There are 16 fingers to the foot.

People under the age of 30 are not considered adults in Ancient Greece.

Slaves are not allowed to use their own names – their owners have the right to rename them.

Unusually, in Athens the police force is made up of slaves.

If you are planning a long visit to Athens, make sure you do not become too powerful or you could face ostracism – banishment from the state for a period of ten years.

Citizens bring to the meeting small pieces of broken pottery called ostraka. On each ostrakon is scratched the name of the person the citizen wants to ostracize.

Every year a meeting is held and citizens are invited to write down the name of the person they most want to get rid of. If enough people write the same man's name, he will be ostracized.

63

❓ Souvenir quiz

Take your time exploring Ancient Greece. It is a fascinating land with plenty to see and experience. Before you leave, test your knowledge with this fun quiz. You will find the answers on page 128.

1. Why do Greeks usually travel by boat rather than going overland?

a) Because there are bandits and thieves lurking on many of the inland roads ready to attack unsuspecting travellers.

b) Because the inland regions are very mountainous and difficult to cross.

c) Because Greeks do not want to upset Poseidon, god of the sea.

2. Why is pale skin considered the height of fashion for Greek women?

a) It shows that they come from such a wealthy and respectable family that they do not need to work outside in the sun.

b) They are worried about the harmful effects of the sun on their skin.

c) Pale skin complements their brightly coloured chitons.

3. Why does Greek furniture often have only three legs?

a) Three-legged furniture can stand more firmly on bumpy earth floors.

b) Wood is scarce in Greece and it is too expensive to make furniture with four legs.

c) The number three has religious importance.

4. How do Greeks show their appreciation at the theatre?

a) By clapping their hands.

b) By shouting at the actors.

c) By whistling and stamping their feet.

5. Who is allowed to speak at an assembly?

a) Anyone in Greece.

b) Any citizen of the city-state of Athens.

c) Aristocrats and important citizens.

6. Spartan men have to do 23 years' military training. Why are Spartan women expected to exercise and keep fit?

a) So that they produce strong, healthy babies.

b) So that they will be ready to fight and defend Sparta against attack.

c) So that they are strong enough to stop the helots (the land slaves that work the fields and cook the food) from rebelling.

7. An assembly is called in Athens roughly every nine days. Who keeps order at the assembly?

a) Officials elected by the assembly each year.

b) The oldest citizens at the assembly.

c) Slave archers wearing special caps and capes.

8. Greeks believe there is a family of gods. Where are the gods believed to live?

a) In the clouds above Mount Olympus.

b) In the Parthenon temple on the Acropolis.

c) In the sea.

9. The Olympic Games are held in Olympia every four years. What prize is presented to the triumphant winners at the Games?

a) A large sum of money.

b) A wreath of olive leaves cut from a sacred tree.

c) A medal made of gold.

10. To find out what the future has in store, Greeks travel to Delphi and consult the oracle. What is the oracle?

a) An ancient prophecy inscribed on tablets of stone.

b) A statue of the god Apollo.

c) A priestess who has the power to speak to the gods.

65

ANCIENT ROME

A GUIDE TO ROME IN AD 128, WHEN HADRIAN WAS EMPEROR

Introducing Rome

Welcome to Rome, greatest city in the world. It is the heart of the largest empire ever seen, ruling over millions of people from places as far apart as Britain and Egypt. Above all it is a city of extremes. Filled with spacious palaces and public buildings, it is also the most crowded site on Earth. One million people live here, crammed into the narrow streets. And although the Empire's riches pour into Rome, over 200,000 people are out of work and rely on the emperor for free grain.

The emperor Hadrian is rarely in Rome itself. He spends years travelling through the Empire, protecting its frontiers and exploring many local cultures. However, he has still found time to organize new building projects in his capital.

According to legend, Rome was founded by Romulus. He and his brother were abandoned here as babies, and cared for by a wolf.

For centuries, Rome was ruled by a senate of important men. SPQR stands for *"the Senate and the People of Rome"*.

Rome's first rival was the African city of Carthage. Its army used elephants to attack Italy, but they were defeated.

Rome's weather is good, and people spend most of the time outdoors.

In the Forum, look for the Rostra platform where political speeches are made.

Rome has grown beyond its walls. Its empire is so strong, it needs no defence.

Rome's spiritual heart is the ancient Roman Forum, or market place. Centuries ago, when Rome was a village, its people met in this open space to trade and discuss politics. Now the old square is built up with giant temples and political memorials, and the markets have moved elsewhere. The old ruling Senate House is still by the Forum, but Rome's real centre of power is now the emperor's palace nearby.

Sightseers' tip
You will see vast differences in wealth here in Rome. A tiny elite is staggeringly rich, but one third of its people are slaves.

For 250 years after beating Carthage, Rome's efficient armies conquered all the lands round the Mediterranean Sea.

A great general, Julius Caesar, destroyed the Senate's power and ruled Rome alone, but he was murdered by the senators.

After Caesar's death, his adopted son Augustus took control. He became the first in a long line of emperors.

Travelling around

You'll have no problem getting to Rome. It is the centre of the finest road system ever constructed. There are over 50,000 kilometres of superb highway covering the Empire, all built by the Roman army. Communications are easier now than at any time in history, and you could cross the Empire in just 100 days on horseback. Once you're in Rome itself, however, it's not always easy finding your way about. None of the thousands of winding streets have names or numbers.

If you can hitch a lift on a merchant ship, a great way to get to Rome is up the River Tiber. Hundreds of small craft sail to and from the coast, bringing grain, wine and other supplies that the city needs.

A new road is given very hard-wearing foundations. A flat layer of sand goes on the bottom, with layers of stone and gravel above. The road is topped with paving stones, which are humped to let rain run off. Road engineers use tools to keep their course as straight as possible, so that all distances are minimized.

On the way to Rome, look out for milestones that tell you how far you've got to go.

If you get lost in the city, use temples and statues as landmarks to find your way.

Take a slave with you if you go out at night. Thieves and muggers are common in Rome.

Sightseers' tip

If you're caught short in the street, look for a urine jar. The contents of these are sold to cloth makers, who use it to dissolve fat and grease left in fresh wool.

Although rich people might travel about by sedan chair, by far the best way to get around Rome is on foot. There are raised pavements to keep you out of the mud and sewage on the roads, and stepping stones to help you cross. Walking also keeps you mobile in the main streets, which stay busy even at night. Traders with noisy, slow-moving carts are only allowed into the city at dusk, and soon block the streets. Traffic jams are common, and so are lost tempers.

71

What to wear

Romans pay a lot of attention to their appearance, and you should fit in with their current styles. For instance, men have traditionally been clean-shaven, but the emperor has just begun a new fashion for wearing beards. Old-style togas are still worn for important occasions, but for day-to-day use, the simpler tunic is now preferred.

Rich women have personal slaves to shape their hair in elaborate styles. This can take all morning. Others wear wigs made from the hair of foreign slaves – blonde hair from German women is thought to be very exotic.

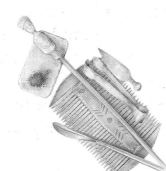

Romans have plenty of tools to help improve their looks. You can invest in combs, hairpins, tweezers for plucking hairs, and special small spoons for scooping wax out of your ears.

You can buy stick-on leather patches to cover any nasty spots or scars.

Men must wear their togas when visiting the law courts or on official business.

Roman women often use crushed ants' egg paste to darken their eyebrows.

Both men and women wear jewellery, including brooches to hold their cloaks in place. Snake bracelets are popular, and so are gold necklaces set with precious stones.

Sightseers' tip For women, a pale face is a sign of status. Poor women have rough, red faces from working in the open. Use creams of chalk, flour and lead to whiten your skin.

A fashionable Roman woman takes great care with her clothes. She first puts on an ankle-length woollen under-tunic, with a colourful embroidered dress, or *stola*, on top. This can be made of wool, cotton or silk. She then places a beautiful jewelled girdle around her waist. Wealthy men wear long tunics. Poorer men and slaves have shorter tunics, which give their legs more freedom as they work.

73

Food and drink

What you eat in Rome will depend on one simple thing: money. If you're rich, you'll taste an unending array of exotic delicacies – from stuffed dormice to ostrich and flamingo. If not, you'll share most people's diet of grain boiled into porridge and mixed with cheap foods like eggs and cheese. For these Romans, meat is a rare dish. Whoever you are, wine mixed with water is the usual drink. It is considered vulgar to drink wine undiluted.

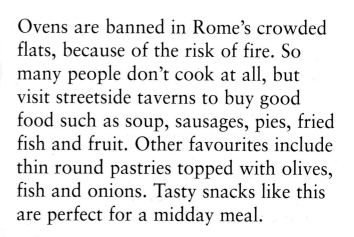

Roman kitchens contain many spices and herbs. Spicy sauces are put on everything to cover the rotting taste of old meat or fish. The favourite sauce is *liquamen*, strained from salted fish guts left out in the sun.

Ovens are banned in Rome's crowded flats, because of the risk of fire. So many people don't cook at all, but visit streetside taverns to buy good food such as soup, sausages, pies, fried fish and fruit. Other favourites include thin round pastries topped with olives, fish and onions. Tasty snacks like this are perfect for a midday meal.

 At some parties, dancing and music is laid on while guests eat.

 Rome is a day's journey from the sea, so fish here is seldom fresh!

 Need a cure for indigestion? Try raw cabbage soaked in vinegar.

Hosts holding parties seek to impress their guests with the very finest silver dishes. Salads and oysters are often brought out for starters, followed by several courses of game birds, boar, venison, hare, ham and fish. Meals end with honey cakes and fruit.

Sightseers' tip

At some big banquets with huge amounts of food, a room is set aside as a *vomitorium* for those who eat too much too soon. By making yourself sick there, you can empty your stomach ready for the next few courses!

At most dinner parties, the guests recline on three couches around a table. They support themselves on the left elbow, and hold their food in the right hand. Knives or spoons are rarely used, so most foods are quite solid and not served too hot. The host's slaves serve everyone, but guests sometimes bring their own slaves along to help out.

Accommodation

There are great differences in the quality of housing in Rome. The city sprawls over seven hills and all the richest people live in spacious villas on the airy higher ground. Everyone else is crammed into ramshackle blocks of flats filling the valleys in between. In summer, these hot, over-crowded streets are a breeding-ground for disease, and the few who can afford it leave the city for the country. Rich or poor, most people don't spend much time at home – they prefer to work and socialize outdoors, or in public places, such as the baths.

Sightseers' tip

Look out for the *vigiles*, Rome's seven squads of professional firemen. Each squad has 1,000 freedmen who tackle fires, and help keep order on the rowdy streets.

Unless you're very rich, you'll have to find lodging in one of the crowded tenement buildings that house most of Rome's people. It is a risky business – the stuffy flats are vulnerable to fire, and are so poorly made that they often fall down. Each block has up to six storeys, with shops on the ground floor. Try for a room at the top – or the noise of traders' carts will keep you awake all night!

People with rooms to let often paint 'For Rent' on the side of the building.

Most houses are airy to keep you cool in summer. In winter, they can be freezing!

The father is head of the family, but his wife runs all household affairs.

A rich man's town house is centred upon the *atrium*, an open hall with a pool in the centre to catch water. Doors to the dining room, reception rooms, kitchen and bedrooms lead off on either side. The *atrium* is the house's main source of light and air – outside walls have few windows, to keep out noise and burglars.
At the back, a *hortus*, or garden, filled with shrubs and statues, provides a tranquil spot for the family to escape the city's hubbub.

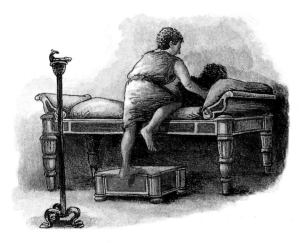

Even big houses don't have much furniture. The couches in the dining room are the most important items. By adding a woolen blanket, they double up as beds at night.

Many houses have small shrines where families worship their own personal gods, called *lares*. Every day, offerings of wine, cakes and incense are made at the shrines, which contain tiny statues of the *lar*. If the offerings are given correctly, the *lar* will bring wealth and happiness to his household.

Shopping

Rome is the most incredible shopping centre on Earth. Every day, ships and wagons arrive from all over the Empire, carrying goods made in distant corners of the world. Traders from as far as India and China bring back luxury silks and spices to delight the wealthy buyers here. But there are countless affordable things to buy too: whether you're after shoes, pots or clothes, you'll find exactly what you want in Rome.

Rome is the richest city in the Empire, and luxury goods are plentiful here. This vase, specially carved out of blue and white glass, would have taken months to make, and can be afforded only by the super-rich.

Most Roman shops are stalls or rooms opening out on to the street. Here you can buy many exotic things: wool from Britain, silver from Spain, carpets from Turkey and perfumes from Iran. But of all the goods on sale, by far the most important are the huge amounts of grain that arrive daily from Africa. Rome is so big that Italian farmers can't supply enough wheat, so imports are essential if the poor are to be kept alive. In hard times, the emperor gives free hand-outs of grain to the needy.

The newest and most spectacular place to browse in Rome is Trajan's Market near the Forum. Made using the latest technology, it is a massive semi-circular shopping centre carved out of the side of a hill, with 150 shops, offices and a central open space where traders can set up their stalls.

 To find a tavern, look for green boughs hanging over the door.

 The same coinage is used across the Empire, from Asia Minor to Britain.

The best mass-produced red pottery comes from France.

Sightseers' tip

If you're a woman, don't be seen shopping for anything other than perfume, jewellery or clothes. Most ordinary shopping is done by male slaves.

Slaves are brought to Rome from battlefields at the edges of the Empire. You can pick them for their strength or looks, or for skills such as dancing, cookery or music. Talented slaves can cost 12 times as much as unskilled ones.

The baths

The public baths are an essential part of life in Rome. There are hundreds of baths in the city, and many people visit one every day to spend a few relaxing hours swimming, chatting or playing games in magnificent surroundings. Most trips to the baths are free, because rich men pay everyone's fees in the hope of gaining votes or increasing their popularity.

For the Romans, personal hygiene is vital. Clean yourself by rubbing oil into your skin, then scraping off the mingled oil and dirt with a blunt metal tool called a *strigil*.

Sightseers' tip

Watch out! Water in steam baths is heated by air from underground furnaces, so the floor tiles are scalding. You may wish to wear sandals to protect your feet.

Hire a slave to guard your clothes – or they might be stolen.

Men and women bathe separately. A bell signals the change-over.

Slaves sell tasty snacks to help you recover after a long swim.

All the baths are very richly decorated. There are intricate mosaics on the floor, rooms are lined with marble pillars, and the ceilings are high and beautifully painted. All this luxury gives even poor people a regular taste of the power and wealth of Rome.

Look out for the splendid public lavatories at the baths. Some can sit 16 people side by side, so you can chat to your friends with ease. This is better than toilets at home, which are often simply pots in the corner.

There are a bewildering variety of rooms in the baths. They include hot and cold pools, steam rooms, saunas and haircutting salons. The largest baths also have forecourts with shops, restaurants and libraries. When you visit, warm up in the gymnasium by wrestling or playing ball games, then make for the *caldarium* – the hottest room of all – to bring yourself out in a cleansing sweat. After a good massage, finish with an invigorating dip in the ice-cold plunge pool.

The theatre

Visiting the theatre is one of the Romans' favourite pastimes. There are several semi-circular stone theatres in the city, hosting plays and games to celebrate recent victories. Shows last many hours, and there are several kinds to see. Although some Greek tragedies are shown, Romans are more keen on comedy, with lots of crude jokes, fast action and happy endings. Some characters are very popular, such as the cunning slave, who always manages to talk himself out of trouble in the nick of time.

Sightseers' tip

Don't hire rooms near a theatre. To get good seats, a crowd will gather the night before a show – and they make a lot of noise. The emperor Caligula once ordered his guards to beat up a crowd after they kept him awake all night!

 Free food and drink is usually provided by the show's sponsor.

 Theatres sometimes bring wild beasts on stage to attract larger crowds.

! For some tragedies, a real-life criminal might be executed live on stage.

Actors rehearse in the building behind the back of the stage. They are all men, but they play many women's roles too.

Romans love special effects – ghosts appear through holes in the stage floor and winches help produce gods from above. There is little scenery, although real chariots and horses can appear on stage. Actors wear standardized masks, wigs and colours to show what kind of character they are playing. If the crowd is pleased, they clap, snap their fingers and thumbs and wave their togas – but if not, they will hiss, shout and make rude noises.

Music and songs accompany many plays. Greek instruments such as the stringed lyre or *cithara* are popular, and so are the double pipes, cymbals and tamborine, which can all be heard well in the open air.

The temples

Religion is an important part of life in Rome. Everything from personal health to success in war depends on the favour of the gods, and regular rituals must be carried out to keep them satisfied. In hundreds of temples across the city, special priests elected from among Rome's nobles perform sacrifices on behalf of the people. Festivals and feast days are held for each god, and offerings of fruit, wine and animals are made each day.

Jupiter is the king of the gods, and Rome itself is under his protection. He also controls the sky and weather. Many other gods watch over every aspect of life. Some of the most important are Mars, the god of war, Apollo, the god of light and music, Vesta, the goddess of home and hearth, and Minerva, the goddess of wisdom.

Sightseers' tip

Want to know your destiny? The Romans are keen on divination – the interpretation of omens. Thunder, lightning and the behaviour of birds are studied and used to predict the future.

Sacred chickens are watched for omens during army campaigns.

 During *Saturnalia*, the winter festival, people give each other presents.

Hadrian is said to have designed the Pantheon's dome himself.

Animal sacrifices are often carried out. Each animal must be a perfect physical specimen, and the more willingly it goes to the slaughter, the better the omen. Once dead, its entrails are studied: if they are in good condition, the body is cooked for the pleasure of the gods.

If you are ill and need a god's help, your prayers must be accompanied by a gift. Leave a model of the sick part of your body at the temple.

The newest and one of the greatest sights in Rome is Hadrian's Pantheon, a temple to all the gods. It is a masterpiece of engineering, with the world's widest dome (43m), made from concrete poured over a temporary wooden framework. Statues of the gods line the walls. A single hole at the top, the *oculus*, provides the only light and represents the sun in the heavens.

Circus Maximus

If there's one unmissable sight in Rome, it's the Circus Maximus. This giant chariot-racing circuit is over 500 years old, and is by far the biggest stadium in the world. Up to 250,000 people can crowd in to watch the races – that's a quarter of Rome's population! Everyone comes here to cheer on their teams and gasp at the high-speed crashes. Entry is free to watch all the day's 24 races.

If you enjoy a flutter – beware! You can bet on chariot races and gladiator fights, but it is illegal at other times. Still, Romans love gambling, and many go to secret betting houses, where they can wager money on dice or on the tossing of coins.

Sightseers' tip Keep an eye out for cheating. Drivers have been known to slip a stick through their rivals' spokes to make them crash.

Races start when an official drops a handkerchief. There are four teams in each race, the blues, whites, reds and greens. Each race lasts for seven 1.5km laps of the wall or *spina* at the centre of the arena.

The Circus is a very popular place for secret meetings between lovers.

Track marshals stand by to throw water on the smouldering wheels of crashed chariots.

Look out for seven dolphins on the *spina*. One is removed to mark each lap.

Chariot racing is popular with all age groups. Children from wealthy families are given small chariots to play in, pulled by donkeys or even goats!

Each chariot is as light and mobile as possible, but they are very flimsy and can easily overturn. The most dangerous parts of the course are the corners. It is very difficult to turn the chariots at high speeds and collisions are common. Drivers try to drive their opponents into the wall. Each driver has only leather thongs to protect his body, and if he does have a "shipwreck" he is likely to be badly injured or killed.

87

The Colosseum

No visitor to Rome should miss the impressive Flavian Amphitheatre – also known as the Colosseum – which can be seen from all over the city. It is the biggest amphitheatre in the world, and can hold a staggering 55,000 spectators. Try to visit on a public holiday, when everyone can get in free to watch the spectacular and bloodthirsty shows that take place there.

Exotic creatures from all over the known world are brought to Rome to appear at the Colosseum. The crowd's favourites are the ferocious lions, which are set loose to devour helpless criminals.

Gladiators are either slaves, prisoners or criminals. If they entertain the crowd they may get gifts of coins, but only those who survive many fights will be set free. These lucky few are given bone tablets with their names on to prove they are now free men.

Don't worry about the huge crowds at the Colosseum – there are 80 entrances, so you'll be able to find a seat quickly. When you are inside, your head will be protected from the strong sun by an enormous canvas awning that can be moved back and forth by teams of slaves pulling on hundreds of ropes outside.

To keep the people happy, there are over 100 public holidays in Rome every year.

Prisoners and wild beasts are kept in a maze of cages under the arena's floor.

Why not place a bet on your favourite gladiator? If he wins his fight, you'll be rich!

Gladiators are the most popular entertainment here. Many fighters come out onto the arena together, and lots are drawn to see which men will fight each other to the death. There are several different types of gladiator, each with their own weapons, armour, strengths and weaknesses.

Many spectators love the brave and nimble *retarius*, who tries to snare his enemy in a net and then stab him with his trident. Others prefer the *secutor*, whose weighty equipment makes him slow but powerful.

Heavy helmets give gladiators protection, but they are difficult to see out of, which is risky when fighting a fast opponent.

Sightseers' tip

Watch for the emperor, as he decides whether a beaten gladiator should live or die. If he gives the thumbs up, the man will live – but if it is thumbs down, he will be killed by his opponent.

Around Rome

Although the city of Rome dominates this part of Italy, it is well worth taking a trip to the beautiful countryside beyond it. The way of life is slower here, but it is crucial to the well-being of the Empire. Much of the land is covered by vast farm estates, owned by the wealthiest men in Rome, which supply much of the food that keeps the city going. Wine and olive oil are the most important crops. They are carried in huge quantities to giant ports on the Mediterranean coast and exported by sea all over the Empire.

Sightseers' tip
Try and buy fresh honey made in one of the estates' beehives. It is the only way to sweeten your food.

Just 25km from Rome at the mouth of the River Tiber, Ostia is the world's busiest port. The emperors have widened its harbour several times to cope with the huge numbers of ships. Massive warehouses on the seafront store grain, wine and olive oil before barges take them up the Tiber to Rome.

Poor quality grapes are made into wine for workers to drink.

Farms are run by the manager, the *vilicus*. He is often a trusted slave.

Although the mild climate is good for crops, the Italian soil is often poor.

Most rich families only visit the estates in the summer to get out of the sweltering city. But there is a workforce of slaves on the farms year-round to tend to the crops and livestock.

A nobleman's villa sits at the heart of each estate, surrounded by houses for slaves and farm workers, market gardens and vineyards. In the autumn, the grapes are picked and crushed by slaves to extract the juice. This is poured into large half-buried jars to ferment and become wine. The jars are sealed with pitch to keep out the rain.

When the olives are harvested from the trees, they are piled into an olive press. Slaves pull the handles down to squash the olives and squeeze the oil out into a jar.

All around Rome, gigantic aqueducts radiate out across the countryside to distant water sources. They supply over 40 million gallons of water to the city every day, mostly to baths and fountains. The water moves by gravity, so each aqueduct must constantly angle downhill along all its length. At the top, stone slabs cover the water channel to keep out dirt.

✔ Survival guide

Rome is a vibrant, cosmopolitan city filled with visitors from lands all over the Empire. It has everything you need to enjoy your stay. However, it is also a place where laws are strictly enforced, and it is vital that you do not fall foul of the authorities, who will punish non-citizens severely for any misdemeanour.

Magistrates are still officially elected to public posts by Rome's citizens. To win support, these rich men will spend massive sums on pleasing the people.

Society

Visitors must be aware of the rigidly defined levels of Roman society. At the top are Roman citizens, who are divided into the wealthy nobility and the ordinary people, or *plebeians*. Non-citizens from outside Rome have fewer rights. Below all these are the slaves, who do most of the work in farm and city. Slaves have almost no rights at all, but they can be freed if their master chooses. Hadrian has just passed a law forbidding masters from killing slaves without a trial.

Administration

The emperor has absolute power. He appoints all the most important officials, who come from the rich nobility. Wealthy young men follow political careers, as lawyers, magistrates, and finally as the governors of far-flung regions of the Empire.

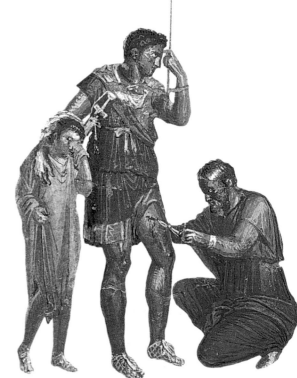

Surgeons have sophisticated tools to operate on wounds and broken bones, but the only pain-killers available are poppy juice and wine.

Non-citizens and slaves who steal from a temple are thrown to wild animals.

To prevent uprisings, the Praetorian Guard is the only legion allowed near Rome.

Romans are tolerant of different religions, but Christians are sometimes persecuted.

Four squads of special legionaries carry out police duties in Rome. In times of serious disturbance, the Praetorian Guard are called in.

Law and Order

The Romans are very keen on discipline and you would be wise not to break their laws during your stay. Minor crimes are punished by beatings. Thieves are branded. For the worst offences, slaves can be executed by crucifixion. An elite force of legionaries, the Praetorian Guard, protects the body of the emperor himself.

Health

Medicine is based largely on herbal remedies and is not always very effective. For broken ribs, for example, the writer Pliny recommends applying a mix of goat's dung and wine to the wound.

Some slaves wear special tags with their master's name and address on. If they run away, they can be caught and returned.

93

？Souvenir quiz

By the time you leave Rome, you will have seen many amazing things. Before you go, find out how much you remember about your visit by trying this special souvenir quiz. The answers are on page 128.

1. The Roman Forum is the most historic site in the city. How did it first start out?

a) As a hilltop fortress.

b) As a market place in a village.

c) As a temple to Romulus, founder of Rome.

2. What kind of creature cared for Romulus as a baby?

a) A wolf.

b) A bear.

c) An eagle.

3. What will keep you awake if you hire a room near street level?

a) Traders' carts bringing goods into the city at night.

b) All-night chariot races through the streets.

c) Drunken revellers on their way home from wild parties.

4. What do fashionable Roman women make wigs out of?

a) Horse hair from Arabian stallions.

b) Human hair from slaves.

c) Finely spun silk from the Far East.

5. Why would a Roman woman want to have a pale face?

a) It proves she's of pure Roman blood.

b) It is considered to be a sign of great health.

c) It proves she is rich enough to stay indoors and not do any work.

6. Precious goods are brought to Rome from all over the known world. But what is Rome's most vital import?

a) Swords from Asia Minor.

b) Grain from Africa.

c) Tea cups from Britain.

7. What is *liquamen*?

a) A mix of rotting fish guts and salt used as a sauce.

b) A strong alcoholic drink made from cranberries.

c) A mix of boars' droppings and wine used to treat bad chest injuries.

8. What equipment does the *retarius* gladiator carry?

a) A weighted net and a trident.

b) A short sword and a heavy rectangular shield.

c) A light javelin and a round shield.

9. The *lares* are very important to most Romans. But who are they?

a) Rome's special fire brigade.

b) The chief priests of Jupiter working at the Pantheon.

c) Household gods who watch over each family.

10. What are "shipwrecks" and where do people go to watch them?

a) Merchant ships running aground in the harbour at Ostia.

b) Rich men's sedan chairs colliding in the Roman Forum.

c) Chariots crashing at the Circus Maximus.

11. Romans love going to the theatre. What kind of play do they most like to see?

a) Greek tragedies, with plenty of death and sorrow.

b) Fast-paced comedies, with lots of farcical situations and silly jokes.

c) Political satires, filled with angry jokes at the emperor's expense.

AZTECS
& INCAS

A GUIDE TO TWO GREAT
AMERICAN EMPIRES IN 1504

Introducing the Aztecs

Visitors to Aztec lands will be rewarded by a truly memorable experience. Although the climate can be harsh, the scenery is stunning and there is plenty to see and do. Most Aztecs live in or near the capital city of Tenochtitlan, built on an island in Lake Texcoco in the central Valley of Mexico in Central America. It will make an ideal base for your holiday.

The central valley is surrounded by high snow-capped peaks. To the southeast, see if you can make out the active volcano Popocatepetl, whose name means 'Smoking Mountain'.

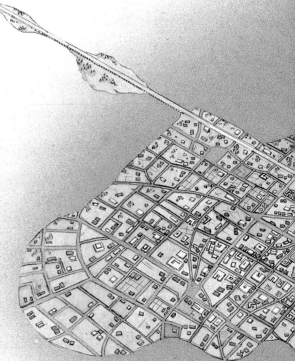

Look out for drawings or carvings of an eagle sitting on a prickly pear cactus, eating a snake. According to legend, this was a sign sent by the god Huitzilopochtli around 175 years ago. It told the Aztecs to settle on the swampy island in Lake Texcoco.

In just under two centuries, Tenochtitlan has grown into a huge, complex city and is now home to around 200,000 people. It is divided into four districts – the Place of the Gods (the temple compound), the Heron's Home, Flowery Meadow and Mosquito Fen, where the local people live and work.

Moctezuma has been the Aztec ruler for two years and is extremely popular with the locals.

To the north of the Valley of Mexico lie dusty deserts. To the south, there are tropical rainforests.

In the Aztec language, Tenochtitlan means 'place of the fruit of the cactus'.

Tenochtitlan is linked to the land by causeways. An aqueduct running parallel to the western causeway brings fresh water to the city from the mountains.

Sightseers' tip

The best time to catch the stunning views of the surrounding mountains and volcanoes is at dawn, before the city is enveloped in a cloud of smoke produced by thousands of cooking fires.

The emperor, or tlatoani, Moctezuma Xocoyotzin lives in the palace at the heart of the city. Parts of the palace were burned in a fire four years ago, so are currently closed for rebuilding works.

Travelling around

Tenochtitlan is made up of an intricate network of canals and waterways, so hiring a canoe to get around is a must. People use boats for everything, whether they are shopping, fishing or just visiting friends and family. Boats vary in size, from a one-person hollowed-out canoe to a larger vessel that takes five people in comfort.

Sightseers' tip

The main canals are bordered by earth pavements, so it is possible to travel by foot in some places. Why not take a leisurely stroll along one of the broad avenues that lead to Moctezuma's palace?

If you can afford it, hire a litter to carry you in style. However, this mode of transport is usually reserved for the tlatoani himself, so be prepared to talk yourself out of trouble if questioned.

As you paddle around the edges of the city, look out for the chinampas, or cultivated gardens. This reclaimed land is shored up by willow twigs and branches and is used to grow fruit, flowers and vegetables. Space in Tenochtitlan is at a premium, so only married couples have the right to live on and farm the chinampas.

Be prepared for lots of walking – the Aztecs do not use wheeled vehicles.

Always keep on the right side of the law. Crimes are punished severely.

Don't expect a nightlife. Ordinary Aztecs believe spirits will steal their souls, if they stay out after dark.

If you are planning a long journey, you could join a trading trip organised by the pochteca, the powerful society of merchants.

Unless you're fit enough to carry your luggage, you'll need to employ a porter. And, be warned, the merchants are so secretive about their business that they make all their excursions under the cover of darkness.

Out and about and desperate for the toilet? Don't worry. Keep an eye out for wicker cabins on city streets or country roads. Human waste is collected from these public lavatories, loaded onto big barges, then transported to the chinampas to be used as fertilizer.

What to wear

In summer, daytime temperatures can soar to 35°C, so it is best to adopt local dress to keep cool. Men and boys should wear a white loincloth, with the option of a plain cloak knotted over one shoulder. Women and girls wear loose tunics over long skirts. Most people go barefoot although warriors, and sometimes nobles, wear sandals.

Ordinary people's clothes are made out of coarse cloth, woven from the maguey cactus. The clothes of the nobility are made of fine cotton, and may be edged with fur, or embroidered around the hem.

Your hairstyle is very important in order to show your place in society. Girls, boys and unmarried women wear their hair long and loose. Married women braid and twist theirs into horns at the sides of their heads. Boys who have captured an enemy soldier can trim their hair to shoulder length. Warriors wear topknots when going to war.

Red cochineal dye for cloth is made from the bodies of tiny crushed insects.

 Strict laws tell nobles and ordinary people what they can and cannot wear.

People believe that wearing jewellery will protect them from harm.

Moctezuma has declared a mini-war with the neighbouring state of Tlaxcala, and at any time you may hear the war drums summoning all males over the age of 15 to battle. Look out for the elite jaguar or eagle knights dressed from head to toe in jaguar skins or feathers. Weapons include axes and clubs called maquahuitl, which are spiked with sharp splinters of glassy obsidian rock.

Brooches and necklaces made of pearls and turquoise are popular, as are lip-plugs, nose-plugs and earrings. Only nobles are permitted to wear gold jewellery.

Sightseers' tip   If you see a woman wearing make-up then it is probably her wedding day. Brides use yellow facepaint and red dye on their lips and teeth.

Food and drink

Most people drink water, but on special occasions pulque, a beer made from the sap of the maguey cactus, is often served. It's best to refuse this potent brew as only the elderly are permitted to touch it.

If the hunting has been good, you may be offered goose, pelican or fresh fish caught from the lake.

If you enjoy spicy food, then you're in for a culinary treat. Try dishes flavoured with hot chillis or, if you can't take the heat, those containing milder sweet peppers or honey. Local staples include tortillas (crisp pancakes), tamales (steamed dumplings), atole (a kind of maize, or sweetcorn, porridge), beans and vegetable stew.

Don't get too friendly with an Aztec family's dog – you may find it served for supper! These small, hairless hounds are kept as family pets, fattened up and eventually eaten.

If you are invited to a noble's house for the evening, you can usually expect turkey, duck and venison. You may also be offered an expensive frothy chocolate drink made from cocoa beans and sweetened with honey and vanilla.

Sightseers' tip Don't drink water from the lake! It has been seriously polluted by the manufacture of whitewash, a thin paint used on houses to reflect the sun's rays, and help keep the rooms inside cool.

Try the local delicacy – green slime skimmed from Lake Texcoco. It tastes a bit like cheese!

Don't expect to use knives, forks or spoons – people eat with their fingers.

 Wondering why chocolate is so pricey? Cocoa beans are also used as money.

If you stay with a local family, you may be asked to lend a hand grinding maize on the stone metlatl. The flour is then shaped into tortillas and fried on a griddle, called a comal.

Accommodation

Staying with a local family is the best option in busy, central Tenochtitlan, but expect to share a room. Most town houses are built around a courtyard, and are home to up to 15 people. In the ordinary thatched cottages on the chinampas, the whole family will live in just one or two rooms.

Every household uses three-legged terracotta bowls to store drinking water or food. In smart homes, these are beautifully decorated.

You'll find top of the range accommodation in the home of a noble family. This type of house has three or four bedrooms, two spacious reception rooms (one for men and one for women) and a kitchen. Meals are served in the dining room, and you'll have servants to wait on you.

Sightseers' tip

Don't worry if you forget to pack your alarm clock. The whole of Tenochtitlan is woken at sunrise by local priests blowing trumpets made from giant conch shells – so there's no danger of oversleeping!

Don't expect a soft, comfy bed. Most people sleep on a reed mat rolled out on the floor.

You should expect just two meals a day – one a few hours after sunrise, the other in the evening.

Food is rationed to one tortilla for children from 3 to 5 years, rising to two for those over 13.

All houses contain a small shrine for the family to worship the gods. Many ordinary people honour the maize goddess, Xilonen.

The houses of the nobility may have one or two storeys. Their shaded balconies, cool fountains and lush gardens make them the ideal place to escape the heat of the midday sun.

After a day's sightseeing, why not take a refreshing steam bath? The mudbrick room is heated by a fire outside. You make the steam by throwing water on the walls inside.

107

Shopping

No visit to Tenochtitlan is complete without a trip to the market. It is incredibly busy, with up to 60,000 traders and visitors each day. Don't worry though, even though it's bustling, it's well organized and divided into areas according to what's on sale, so it's easy to find your way round.

Sightseers' tip If you think you're being cheated or you need help in some way, make for the long, open-sided hall in the middle of the market. Officials there will settle any disputes.

The noise from the market can be heard five kilometres away.

Most goods are bartered, but cocoa beans or quills filled with gold dust are also used as money.

Look out for doctors tending their patients at the market. Herbs are sold as remedies.

One of the most fragrant parts of the market is that devoted to flowers. Also look out for heaps of spices and the brilliantly-coloured feathers used to edge robes or make headdresses.

Whatever souvenirs you want to buy, you'll find them at the market! Look out for cheap, locally-made sandals, woven cloth, baskets and ceramics. Goods brought in from further afield, such as shells from the coast, jade or turquoise, are more pricey. If you're tired of shopping and bartering, you can stop for a snack, have your hair cut, or get your fortune told.

If you're interested in a craft, such as featherworking or ceramics, why not visit the craftspeople at work? They belong to guilds and work in different areas of the city. Ask a local for directions.

Avoid getting mixed up in the part of the market where slaves are sold. Some slaves are prisoners who have been captured in war. Others may be Aztec people who have committed a crime and lost their freedom.

Sports and leisure

If you're a sports enthusiast, make sure you take in a game of tlachtli during your visit. It is fast-paced and tough – and very popular with the spectators. Not only is it exciting to watch, but tlachtli has religious significance too, standing for the battle between darkness and light. The ball symbolizes the Moon and the Sun, and the court represents the world.

On most street corners, you can see locals playing the gambling game of patolli. Players move coloured counters across the board according to the throw of marked, numbered beans.

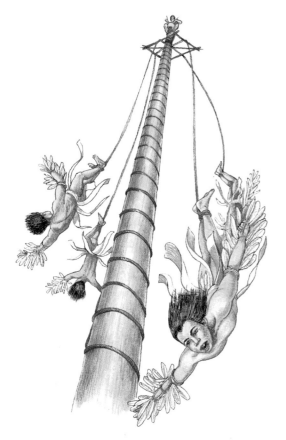

Depending on what time of year you visit, you may be able to see the flying festival in which four men dressed as birds leap from a high pole to honour the gods.

In tlachtli, it is forbidden for hands or feet to touch the solid rubber ball – only hips and knees can be used. The battle between the two teams to score the most hoops is long and hard. Some of the players may have bet all their possessions on the game.

Hundreds of people take part in dances held on important feast days.

After school, children must attend religious school to learn music and dance.

In tlachtli, the losing team may sometimes be sacrificed to the gods.

If sport isn't your thing, you could go to a concert or take part in a feast-day dance. Aztec musical instruments include flutes, bells and rattles.This teponaztli, or two-toned wooden drum, has a decorative owl carving on its side.

Sightseers' tip

Be prepared to lose your cloak, if you go to a ball game. Winning teams may be entitled to take the spectators' clothes and belongings!

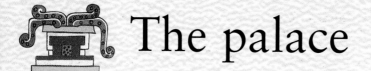

The palace

The royal palace has up to 500 visitors each day, who come to present tribute (a form of tax) to the tlatoani. Only rulers and nobles are allowed into the palace, but if you are lucky you may be invited as a guest. Don't expect to see Moctezuma himself though, even if you're in the same room. It is forbidden to look directly at him.

The day-to-day running of the empire is carried out by the tlatoani's deputy, Cihuacoatl, and hundreds of other officials.

Scribes keep the palace records in folding books called codices. Instead of writing, they use picture symbols, known as glyphs. All tribute goods presented to the emperor, such as jade necklaces, honey, headdresses or blankets, are documented.

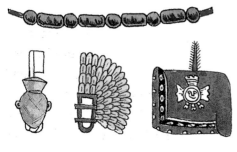

Parts of the palace are currently being rebuilt because of a flood four years ago.

Cihuacoatl means 'Snake Woman', but the job is always done by a man.

The palace's rooms are richly painted and decorated with gold and silver.

The palace is huge and there is too much to see in a single day. It has thousands of rooms, including dining halls, libraries and lawcourts, and even a secret treasure house. There are also separate apartments for women, for the ruler's many wives, and for his 3,000 servants.

Sightseers' tip

Try to fit in a tour of the palace's magnificent gardens and zoo. The zoo contains many exotic and rare creatures, including quetzal birds, whose long, brilliantly-coloured plumes are prized by featherworkers.

All the neighbouring towns and cities conquered by the Aztecs must send tribute to the emperor. If they fail to do so, they face attack by his powerful army.

Place of the Gods

If you are feeling brave, visit the main temple complex in the heart of Tenochtitlan. Dominated by the Great Temple pyramid, it consists of several temples, as well as the priests' living quarters. However, make sure you avoid being in the complex when the Aztecs make their sacrifices to the gods.

Sightseers' tip

Don't faint if you see Aztecs pricking their fingers with the spine of a cactus to draw blood. People leave the spines in their local temple as offerings to the Sun god.

The Aztecs believe that human sacrifice keeps their gods happy, and so prevents the world from ending. During times of sacrifice, the steps of the Great Temple are drenched in the blood of the victims killed on altars at the top.

Look out for one of the thousands of priests that live in the temple complex. They are easy to spot as they blacken their faces with soot and do not cut their hair. You may well want to give them a wide berth as they are the people who perform the sacrifices.

 Look out for the gruesome rack of skulls which stands in the complex.

The Aztecs need to be at war constantly in order to supply the priests with prisoners for sacrifice.

 The Great Temple has been enlarged many times. It is now 30 metres tall.

Steep steps at the front of the Great Temple lead to twin shrines at the top, dedicated to Tlaloc, the god of rain and fertility, and Huitzilopochtli, the god of the Sun and war. Each shrine houses a huge gold statue of the god, and the walls are richly decorated with carvings and paintings.

The Aztec people celebrate small local fiestas throughout the year. Try to attend a ceremony to celebrate the birth of a baby. It will be a joyful occasion with plenty of music and dancing.

Don't miss seeing the Stone of the Sun. This calendar measures the Aztec year, which is 360 days long, with five unlucky days at the end. At the centre is the face of the Sun god.

115

Introducing the Incas

For a change of scene, take a trip to Peru in South America to the empire of the Inca people. Be prepared to ford rivers and hack through tropical forests. Once you reach Inca lands, however, getting around is easy due to the well-maintained roads. The Incas' network of highways connects this vast empire, even allowing easy access to the high Andes mountains.

If you run short of supplies on the road, look out for a storehouse. These buildings are run by the government, and hold food and clothing for people in times of need.

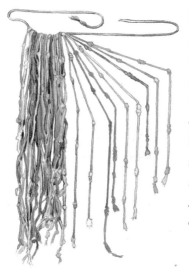

If you need to send a message, enlist the help of a quipocamayo, someone trained in making and reading quipus. These knotted bundles of coloured string can record all sorts of information. A runner will carry it anywhere in the empire.

Although Incas are very hardy, even they find it chilly in the mountains. You will need a poncho made from llama wool, and a knitted cap.

Sightseers' tip It's advisable to hire a llama to carry your bags on the steep mountain roads. Don't drive it too hard though, or it will sit down, refuse to move and spit!

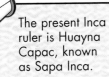 The present Inca ruler is Huayna Capac, known as Sapa Inca.

 Avoid travelling in spring because of flash floods in the mountains.

Ordinary people are often made to work on building projects all over the empire.

Be ready to pay a toll to cross one of the many suspension bridges that you will encounter. Although they may be shaky, they are cleverly constructed and quite safe!

The golden city

During the great festival in December, hundreds of gold and silver objects are buried as sacrifices to the Sun god.

At the heart of the Inca empire lies Cuzco, the administrative and religious capital. If you plan to stay in the city, make sure to dress in the finest clothes and wear plenty of gold and silver jewellery, because only rich and important people live here. Your first stop in Cuzco should be the magnificent Temple of the Sun. With its gold-plated walls and a huge image of Inti, the Sun god, at its centre, it makes an awesome sight.

Take a walk to the area of Cuzco where the master goldsmiths live, and you can watch precious metals being worked into jewellery and ornaments. First the metal is melted, then it is poured into moulds. Finally, with great skill, it is beaten and soldered into shape.

Sightseers' tip

Don't forget that Cuzco is in an earthquake zone. If a building starts to shake, stand under the door lintel and don't panic – Inca houses are built to survive even severe tremors. The stones may move, but they won't collapse.

Alongside the Sun Temple is the Golden Garden. This stunning attraction contains life-sized models of animals and plants, all made from pure gold. You might even spot the Sapa Inca and his wives there.

Incas call gold 'sweat of the Sun' and silver 'tears of the Moon'.

The streets of Cuzco are laid out in the shape of a puma, a sacred Inca animal.

Listen out for the delicate notes made by the panpipes, a popular Inca musical instrument.

The Incas are expert builders. Temples, forts and houses are made from large stone blocks, each shaped to fit together perfectly. Workers pull the blocks up ramps on wooden rollers, then lever them into place with long poles.

Outpost of the empire

Venture north from Cuzco into the Andes and you'll reach Machu Picchu, a spectacular fortress city carved into the side of a mountain. The best way to experience life in this isolated outpost is to stay with a local farming family in their stone cottage. The accommodation will be basic though, as most homes have just one room, shared by the whole family.

Don't trip over a guinea pig when you step inside an Inca home. They are fattened up on scraps, then end up in the pot themselves.

Inca women work hard, all day long. When not labouring in the fields, they must weave all their family's cloth on a backstrap loom.

Sightseers' tip

Every family must give a proportion of the cloth and food they produce to the government as a kind of tax.

You may get fed up with potatoes by the end of your trip. Mountain people eat them at nearly every meal.

Everyone in Machu Picchu gets up early to tend their maize, quinoa (a type of grain) and other crops. Each family must work on their ruler's fields as well as their own. They also assist their neighbours when a crop needs planting or harvesting. As only the sons of nobles go to school, most children spend the day helping their parents – gathering herbs, herding llamas or carrying firewood.

 Ordinary people have little furniture, so be prepared to sleep on the floor.

 Important religious festivals are held at the beginning of each growing season.

Inca nobles are wealthy and live in well-built houses with plenty of servants.

Terraces are cut into the hillside to make level fields for the crops.

As a rule, most Inca people are law-abiding and hardworking. Every household shares a leader with 10–15 other families. The leaders report to local rulers, who report to provincial governors. They, in turn, report to one of four governors who answer to the Sapa Inca himself.

Survival guide

To keep things running smoothly and to closely control their large empires, both Aztec and Inca societies are highly-organized and strict. There is a great deal of bureaucracy, and you will need permission to travel anywhere. But although life is often tough for ordinary citizens, you will notice that few people are hungry or homeless.

Law and order

Laws are harsh and law-breakers are severely punished. The penalty for many crimes is death. In Aztec society, first offenders may lose their home. If they commit the same crime again, they are killed.

Badly behaved Aztec children are sometimes held over a fire containing chilli peppers. This harsh punishment hurts their throats and makes their eyes stream.

Health

Both Aztec and Inca doctors use a mixture of herbal medicine and common sense to heal the sick. If you fall ill, though, be careful. Some herbal drugs are quite dangerous and kill rather than cure. Inca doctors also rely on prayers and charms to cure patients, and often conduct healing rituals in the cold mountain rivers.

Before you travel, consult an Aztec priest to see whether the day is lucky or unlucky.

Inca men always carry with them a small bag containing a lucky charm.

If a member of a calpulli breaks the law, the whole calpulli may be punished.

The coca plant is more highly valued by the Incas than gold and silver. They believe it has sacred powers and often burn it in temples. The leaves are also chewed to give a person energy or to overcome nausea.

Administration

Aztec towns and cities are divided into calpullis, or clans. Tenochtitlan alone has about 80 calpullis. Each calpulli is responsible for its own part of the city. It has its own temple and school, and makes sure the streets are swept every day and the sewage removed. It also cares for the sick and elderly.

Even though they have many laws, the Aztecs believe it is their gods who ultimately rule their lives. They try to positively influence the gods by giving gifts and offering them sacrifices.

❓ Souvenir quiz

Your trip to the Aztec lands in the Valley of Mexico and the Inca empire in the Andes is over. Try this souvenir quiz to see how much you can remember from your visit. You will find the answers on page 128.

1. What does the name of the Aztec's main city, Tenochtitlan, mean in the Aztec language?

a) Eagle eating a snake.

b) The lands beside the water.

c) Place of the prickly pear cactus.

2. Why should you not get too friendly with an Aztec family's dog?

a) It may be sacrificed at the top of the Great Temple in the centre of Tenochtitlan.

b) You may be upset if it ends up in the family's stewing pot and is served for supper.

c) You may be made to breathe smoke from a fire containing chilli peppers as a punishment.

3. How do you take a bath, Aztec-style?

a) You sit in one of the wicker cabins lining the city streets and roads.

b) You jump off a chinampa into Lake Texcoco and scrub yourself all over with green slime and maize flour.

c) You sit inside a mudbrick room while someone stokes the fire outside. Water poured on the walls makes the steam rise.

4. Which goods on sale at the market are probably the most expensive?

a) Locally made sandals and woven cloth.

b) Food grown on the chinampas, such as maize, tomatoes and peppers.

c) Shells and semi-precious stones.

5. What does the Aztec word tlachtli describe?

a) A flying festival in which four men leap from a high pole to honour the gods.

b) A fast-paced ball game in which two teams try to knock a ball through a stone ring.

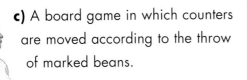

c) A board game in which counters are moved according to the throw of marked beans.

6. How do Aztec girls wear their hair?

a) Trimmed to their shoulders then tied in a topknot.

b) Long and loose.

c) Plaited then twisted into horns at the sides of their heads.

7. What is an Aztec calpulli responsible for?

a) Keeping order and settling disputes at the market.

b) Looking after a particular district or part of a city.

c) Sacrificing victims at the Great Temple in the centre of Tenochtitlan.

8. What is an Inca quipu?

a) A knotted message or record.

b) A kind of string bag carried by Inca men to store the leaves of the coco plant and a lucky charm.

c) A beaded necklace worn by nobles during important festivals in the Golden Courtyard in the capital city of Cuzco.

9. What should you do if there's an earthquake during your stay in the Andes?

a) Stay indoors.

b) Stand in a doorway.

c) Make for the Golden Garden.

10. What do the Incas value more highly than 'sweat of the Sun' and 'tears of the Moon'?

a) The leaves of the coco plant.

b) Gold and silver metalwork.

c) The work of the ordinary people in the fields.

Index

Answers to souvenir quizzes

Ancient Egypt souvenir quiz, pages 34 and 35

1 = c)   2 = b)   3 = b)   4 = a)   5 = c)   6 = c)   7 = b)   8 = a)

Ancient Greece souvenir quiz, pages 64 and 65

1 = b)   2 = a)   3 = a)   4 = c)   5 = b)   6 = a)   7 = c)   8 = a)   9 = b)   10 = c)

Ancient Rome souvenir quiz, pages 94 and 95

1 = b)   2 = a)   3 = a)   4 = b)   5 = c)   6 = b)   7 = a)   8 = a)   9 = c)   10 = c)   11 = b)

Aztecs and Incas souvenir quiz, pages 124 and 125

1 = c)   2 = b)   3 = c)   4 = c)   5 = b)   6 = b)   7 = b)   8 = a)   9 = b)   10 = a)

Acknowledgements

Design assistance
Joanne Brown

Ancient Greece and Ancient Rome consultant
David Nightingale M.A. (Oxon) teaches Greek and Roman history at the University of Kent at Canterbury. He is a regular visitor to Greece and Italy.

Inklink Firenze illustrators
Simone Boni, Alain Bressan, Theo Caneschi, Luigi Critone, Concetta D'Amato, Federico Ferniani, Lucia Mattioli, Francisco Petracchi, Lorenzo Pieri, Alessandro Rabatti

Additional illustrators
Julian Baker, Richard Berridge, Vanessa Card, Peter Dennis, Francesca D'Ottavi, Terry Gabbey, Luigi Galante, Ian Jackson, Nicki Palin, Mark Peppe, David Salariya/Shirley Willis, Thomas Trojer, Richard Ward

Picture credits
b = bottom, c = centre, l = left, r = right, t = top
p.8c The Ancient Egypt Picture Library; p.11cr AKG/Erich Lessing; p.12c Egyptian Museum, Cairo/AKG/Erich Lessing; p.18cl Kunsthistoriches Museum, Vienna/AKG/Erich Lessing; p.21cr E.T. Archive/British Museum; p.23t E.T. Archive/British Museum; p.24bl E.T. Archive/Louvre Paris; p.26bc and b The Ancient Egypt Picture Library; p32c Rockefeller Museum, Jerusalem (IDAM)/AKG/Erich Lessing; p.32bl E.T. Archive/Egyptian Museum, Cairo; p.38c British Museum/Michael Holford; p.40bl Vienna Kunsthistoriches Museum/AKG London; p.43tr British Museum/Michael Holford; p.45tr Ancient Art and Architecture, tl Corbis UK/Araldo de Luca; p.49c AKG London; p.47c British Museum; p.50tr Ancient Art and Architecture; p.53cr American School of Classical Studies, Athens; p.55tr British Museum/Michael Holford; p.56tl Corbis UK/Robert Gill; p.57tl British Museum/Michael Holford; p.59tr British Museum/Michael Holford; p.60tl AKG London/Erich Lessing; p.62cr British Museum/Michael Holford; p.63tr Corbis UK/Gianni Dagli Orti; p.68cl The Bridgeman Art Library, London/New York/Museo Archeologico Nazionale, Naples; p.70cl AKG London/Erich Lessing; p.73tr The British Museum, c Scala; p.75tr The Bridgeman Art Library, London/New York/Louvre, Paris, France; p.78c Ancient Art & Architecture; p.77br The British Museum; p.81tr Ancient Art and Architecture; p.83tl Ancient Art and Architecture; p.84bl C M Dixon/British Museum; p.87tl Giraudon/Louvre, Paris; p.89cr AKG London/Museum für Deutsche Geschichte, Berlin; p.91cr AKG London/Erich Lessing; p.92br Scala; p.98cl Werner Forman Archive; p.103cr Werner Forman Archive/National Museum of Anthropology, Mexico City; p.104tl Corbis; p.106cl The Bridgeman Art Library/Museum für Völkerkunde, Berlin; p.107tr The Bridgeman Art Library/Museo Nacional de Antropologia, Mexico/Giraudon; p.109tl Hutchison Library/Liba Taylor; p.111tl Werner Forman Archive/British Museum; p.113tr NHPA/Kevin Schafer; p.115br Werner Forman Archive/National Museum of Anthropology; p.120tr South American Pictures/Tony Morrison, bl Still Pictures/Edward Parker; p.123tl Still Pictures/Julio Etchart, cr Still Pictures

Every effort has been made to trace the copyright holders of the photographs. The publishers apologise for any inconvenience caused.